THE LIBRARY OF WEAPONS OF MASS DESTRUCTION™

Weapons of Mass Destruction and North Korea

TRACIE EGAN

The Rosen Publishing Group, Inc., New York

Published in 2005 by The Rosen Publishing Group, Inc.
29 East 21st Street, New York, NY 10010

First Edition

Library of Congress Cataloging-in-Publication Data

Egan, Tracie.
Weapons of mass destruction and North Korea / by Tracie Egan.
    p. cm. — (The library of weapons of mass destruction)
Includes bibliographical references and index.
ISBN 1-4042-0296-X (library binding)
1. Weapons of mass destruction—Korea (North)—Juvenile literature.
2. United States—Military policy—Juvenile literature. 3. World
politics—21st century.
I. Title. II. Series.
U793.E345 2004
358'.3'095193—dc22

                                                          2004014692

Manufactured in the United States of America

On the cover: Spent fuel rods in a cooling pond at North Korea's
Yongbyon nuclear facility

[CONTENTS]

INTRODUCTION

N orth Korea is a small country in a remote part of the world. Some people, including many of its own citizens, would say that it is not even a whole country, just half of one. It is not rich, and it has no large stores of important natural resources, such as oil, coveted by other countries, which would allow it to wield worldwide influence. Indeed, it has difficulty even conducting foreign trade, for it has virtually nothing that other countries want. In recent years, it has not even been able to feed its own population without outside help. It attracts few tourists, and, in fact, its strange and brutal ruling

One million people rally in support of North Korea's withdrawal from the Nuclear Non-Proliferation Treaty on January 10, 2003. The rally, occurring at Pyongyang Square the day after the withdrawal, features portraits of the only two leaders the Communist nation has known: the late Kim Il Sung *(left)* and his son, Kim Jong Il *(right)*, North Korea's current leader.

dynasty of "maximum leaders" has generally sought to keep its borders closed to outsiders. Even international aid organizations, such as the Red Cross, have a hard time gaining access. North Korea takes little part in international affairs and has very few allies. Even in today's so-called information age, an era of unprecedented capacity for the exchange of information, few people know anything about North Korea at all.

Not even those whose business it is to know—journalists, diplomats, intelligence agencies, world leaders—could say too many things with certainty about what exactly goes on inside the mystifying, shadowy, and isolated realm that is the Democratic People's Republic of Korea, or North Korea as it is more simply known to the rest of the world.

Yet, every few years, it seems North Korea makes the rest of the world stand up and take notice, provoking a crisis that draws the close and immediate attention of some of the world's richest and most powerful nations and often ends with those nations agreeing to give North Korea much of what it is demanding. Through such times of what some experts have characterized as a kind of blackmail, this pariah among nations becomes a focus of world attention. This otherwise insignificant nation becomes much more than an irritant; it becomes what the United States has recently characterized as a dangerously unpredictable rogue state that is part of nothing less than an international "axis of evil."

What enables this periodic transformation of North Korea's status among the nations of the world? Is it weapons of mass destruction, or, to be more exact, simply the rumor or possibility of their existence within this little-known realm? As with so much else regarding this curious country, there is much mystery surrounding this issue. In the end, it may be this mystery that is North Korea's best weapon of all. Certainly, it enables North Korea to continue commanding a type of attention that the world would otherwise be unwilling to give it, and that, under other circumstances, it has demonstrated it is content to live without. ■

"North Korea is a regime arming with missiles and weapons of mass destruction, while starving its citizens," stated President George W. Bush in his January 29, 2002, State of the Union address at the United States Capitol. After describing the terrorist regimes in North Korea, Iraq, and Iran, the president said, "States like these . . . constitute an axis of evil, arming to threaten the peace of the world. By seeking weapons of mass destruction, these regimes pose a grave and growing danger."

AXIS OF EVIL

In January 2002, U.S. president George W. Bush gave his first State of the Union address. An American political tradition, the State of the Union began as a personal speech from the president to Congress, delivered at the Capitol. In the modern era, the State of the Union address is still given by the president to Congress at the Capitol, but it is also delivered simultaneously to the American people, via nationwide television and radio broadcast.

As its name suggests, the State of the Union message is intended to be an opportunity for the president to present Congress and the nation with his assessment of how the country is faring—the challenges that face it, his plans for meeting them, new programs he may have in mind, proposals to Congress for possible new legislation, and so forth. If the country is at war or facing another kind of foreign crisis, the president may take this chance to update the electorate about how the war is progressing and to inform the people about any new developments, the status of peace negotiations, and the like. If the country is having economic difficulties, the president may use the State of the Union to reassure the people about the future and to introduce programs to lessen their hardship.

UNPRECEDENTED DANGERS

On that Tuesday night, January 29, President Bush had all these things on his mind, as he made clear at the opening of his speech: "Mr. Speaker, Vice President Cheney, members of Congress, distinguished guests, fellow citizens, as we gather tonight, our nation is at war, our economy is in recession, and the civilized world faces unprecedented dangers."

As the president continued, it was clear that war and national security were the foremost subjects on his mind. This was not surprising. A little bit more than three months earlier, on September 11, 2001, the United States had endured an event unlike any in its history. On the morning of that day, four small teams of Islamic militants, associated with a fundamentalist Islamic terrorist group known as Al Qaeda, succeeded in hijacking four separate passenger jets and intentionally crashed the jets into preselected targets. Two of the planes crashed into the Twin Towers of the World Trade Center in New York City. Another flew into the Pentagon complex outside of Washington, D.C., the headquarters of the U.S. Department of Defense and thus the symbol of U.S. military power. Aboard the fourth, passengers struggled with the hijackers as the plane crashed into the countryside of western Pennsylvania.

> "As we gather tonight, our nation is at war . . . and the civilized world faces unprecedented dangers."
>
> *President George W. Bush*

PAKISTAN AND NORTH KOREA:
A TROUBLING FRIENDSHIP

Abdul Qadeer Khan is revered in Pakistan for helping to make the nation a nuclear state. After confessing to selling nuclear proliferation packages to North Korea, Libya, and Iran, he was pardoned by the Pakistani government.

Although an important ally of the United States for years, Pakistan fits many of the U.S. criteria for a rogue state. It is a Muslim nation whose population is moving toward Islamic fundamentalism. Its government has been a frequent sponsor of terrorism, particularly against its neighbor and ally, India. It was a supporter of the Taliban movement in Afghanistan, and it has developed weapons of mass destruction outside of international control and exported WMD technology to the nations the United States considers the "axis of evil" — Iran, Iraq, and North Korea.

Between 1998 and 2002, Abdul Qadeer Khan, a metallurgist who was the head of Pakistan's nuclear weapons program, sold North Korea and other states a "complete package" of nuclear information and raw materials. According to Khan, he made such sales illegally, for personal profit, without the knowledge of the Pakistani government. On other occasions during that time, Pakistan's government traded nuclear technology with North Korea in exchange for missiles.

Although Khan claims that he was shown three actual nuclear weapons while visiting North Korea, U.S. analysts are skeptical of that claim. They do believe, however, that the actions of Khan and Pakistan have greatly aided North Korea's ability to enrich uranium, which brought North Korea that much closer to developing a viable nuclear weapon.

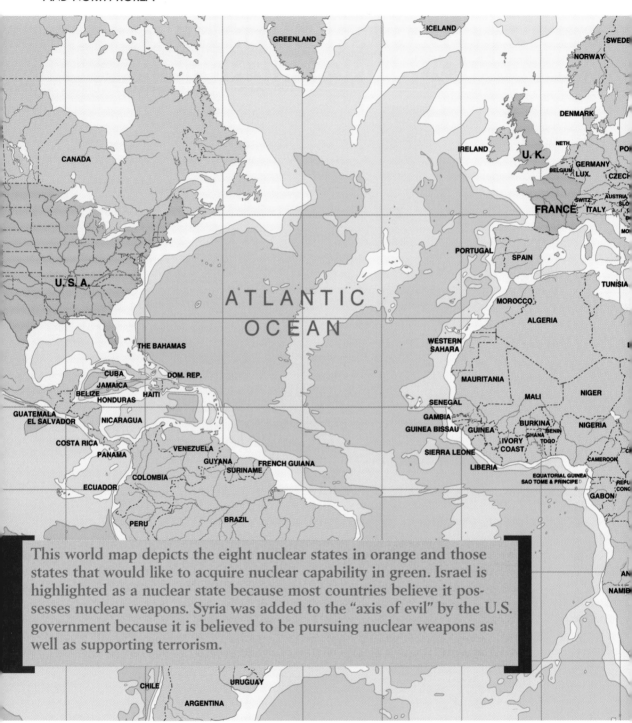

This world map depicts the eight nuclear states in orange and those states that would like to acquire nuclear capability in green. Israel is highlighted as a nuclear state because most countries believe it possesses nuclear weapons. Syria was added to the "axis of evil" by the U.S. government because it is believed to be pursuing nuclear weapons as well as supporting terrorism.

The damage was catastrophic. Everyone aboard all four airliners—265 people in all—was killed. At the Pentagon, 125 Defense Department staffers were killed. More than 2,600 people, including hundreds of firefighters, police, and rescue workers, were killed at the World Trade Center.

FORTUNATE GEOGRAPHY

In the aftermath of the tragedy, the world suddenly seemed a much different, much more dangerous place for most Americans. For the most part, geography and history have served to safely isolate the territory of the United States from the risk of direct attacks from others. Since the early nineteenth century, the United States has stretched the entire breadth of the North American continent, from the Atlantic Ocean to the Pacific Ocean. It has only two foreign neighbors—Canada, which has been a close friend and ally throughout its entire life as a nation, and Mexico. Since Mexico's defeat by the United States in the Mexican-American War (1846–1848) and the resulting loss of territory that now constitutes most of the states of the American Southwest, it has never been strong enough to pose a threat to U.S. interests, even if it wanted to.

No other nation of modern times, with the possible exception of the island nation of Great Britain, has been so fortunate in its geography. Since the War of 1812, the United States has been able to live without any real fear of foreign invasion or attack, a privilege that few other countries have ever known for so long a time. Even the deadly surprise Japanese attack on Pearl Harbor, Hawaii, on December 7, 1941, which brought about the U.S. entry into World War II (1939–1945), occurred on a naval base at a U.S. territory, not yet a state, several thousand miles west of the U.S. mainland.

THE WORLD ON NOTICE

The most important part of President Bush's message to the American people that January evening was that they needed to be aware, if they were not already, that the world was rapidly changing, in a way that affected their security. In the immediate aftermath of the September 11 terrorist attacks, the United States had gone to war with the impoverished, remote central Asian nation of Afghanistan, where the Taliban had been harboring the leadership of Al Qaeda. However, the president had another war in mind that night besides the immediate conflict in Afghanistan. That battle, the president had made clear earlier, was intended as just the first blow in a much larger war—the war on terror. This war, Bush warned, was likely to be lengthy, costly, and open-ended, and it was likely to bring the United States to war against enemies in places that at the present could not be clearly foreseen.

In carrying out this war, the United States was not limiting itself simply to aggressive action against terrorist groups, which almost by definition are small, fluid, clandestine, and stateless. The United States was putting the world on notice that it reserved the right to act also against those countries and governments, like Afghanistan, that offered such groups sanctuary or financial, political, or moral support or encouragement.

ROGUE STATES

There were, Bush believed, a number of rogue states operating in the world that had to be brought into line. These rogue states, the administration argued, were characterized by an aggressive disregard for world opinion, contempt for treaties and international agreements, hatred for the United States, and irresponsible, hostile, and even reckless behavior toward their neighbors and their own people, including support for worldwide terrorism.

That night, in his State of the Union address, President Bush singled out three rogue states in particular—Iraq, Iran, and North Korea. Those three, he said, constituted an "axis of evil" that was "arming to threaten the peace of the world." They had in common one other thing that made them, in Bush's words, "a grave and growing danger." All three, he said, possessed or were seeking to possess weapons of mass destruction, or WMD. ■

2

A COLD WAR
RELIC

Without some understanding of history, it would be difficult to comprehend why North Korea would be a focus of the United States' concerns at the time of President Bush's first State of the Union address. The immediate threat to the national security of the United States that the president spoke about seemed to arise in the Middle East, in the clash of interests involving the United States and its ally Israel; in strategic concerns over the ultimate control of oil, the precious natural resource of the Middle East; and in the grievances addressed and articulated by Islamic fundamentalists.

North Korea is an east Asian state, as far removed geographically as possible from those issues in the Middle East. It is officially an atheist nation, with no concern or involvement in the long, bitter, and bloody historic conflict among Christianity, Islam, and Judaism. It produces no oil of its own and has no natural resources of strategic importance or interest to the United States. It was not guilty, even by association, with involvement in or encouragement of the 9/11 attacks. What, then, made President Bush include it with Iraq and Iran as the so-called axis of evil in the world?

The answer is that North Korea is a kind of relic, a survivor of an earlier period in world history, the Cold War, that many Americans assumed was over and done with, replaced by other significant and escalating troubled spots in the world, such as the Middle East. To understand the antagonism between the United States and North Korea and why the United States should feel so threatened by the prospect of North Korea developing weapons of mass destruction, one must understand a little bit of that Cold War history.

THE COLD WAR

For approximately forty-five years after the last days of World War II, U.S. foreign policy was determined by the demands of the Cold War. The Cold War refers to the political, military, and economic rivalry between the United States and the Soviet Union. These two nations were allies during World War II, and they ended that conflict victorious, as the two most powerful states in the world.

But their friendship had been brief, borne entirely of the mutual need to defeat Nazi Germany before it succeeded in its plans of conquering virtually all of Europe. When the war was over, however, and Adolf Hitler's Nazi regime in Germany had been destroyed, the issues that

A North Korean prisoner of war is being marched at gunpoint by a South Korean policeman during the Korean War. Before this war, the United States had been wary of involvement in Asia. After the United States indicated that it considered Korea to be outside of its defense parameter, the Communist north seized the opportunity to attack the south. The UN was quick to respond and asked the United States for help, beginning a U.S. presence that continues today.

The Big Three, seated left to right, Great Britain's prime minister Winston Churchill, U.S. president Franklin D. Roosevelt, and Soviet premier Joseph Stalin, gathered at the Yalta Conference in February 1945, to prepare for the defeat of Germany. This meeting is often cited as the beginning of the Cold War, as Roosevelt was accused by critics of giving up Eastern Europe to Stalin. Roosevelt died of a cerebral hemorrhage two months later, and Harry Truman would see the United States to the end of the war.

divided the United States and the Soviet Union remained greater than any desire the two countries might have had for increased cooperation. At the end of the war, both the United States and the Soviet Union found themselves with new foreign responsibilities and interests, and each nation discovered that its continued power and prosperity depended on its ability to exert influence outside its own borders, usually at the expense of the other country.

CAPITALISM VERSUS COMMUNISM

The fundamental difference between the United States and the Soviet Union was that of political and economic ideology and practice. The United States was, and is, a democratic, capitalist society. Its government is elected by U.S. citizens and is made up of candidates from different political parties, and its economic system is based on private ownership, in which property rights rest with individuals. These property rights are considered a fundamental right of every citizen. In theory, the government is to play a minimal role in a capitalist system. Its primary role is to mediate and regulate competing economic interests. Economic competition, however, is seen as a good and healthy contribution to the overall strength of the economy and society.

The Soviet Union was a Communist society, meaning that it was governed by a single political party, the Communist Party, and that there was no such thing as private ownership of property. In theory, in a Communist society, all private ownership of property is abolished. Instead, all property is to be owned communally, or jointly, by all citizens of the state. Rather than the

> "From each according to their means, to each according to their needs."
>
> *Communist motto*

economy forming itself from the competition for property and wealth among individuals, as in a capitalist society, the Communist economy is centrally directed by the government. Originally, Communists believed that Communism was the next logical and inevitable evolution of a society after it had reached capitalism—that Communism was a higher state in which the differences between rich and poor and the various social classes have been eliminated in favor of mutual cooperation and a

This poster features philosopher and social theorist Karl Marx. Marx believed that Communism was the last stage of a natural evolution of society that followed capitalism and Socialism, respectively. This theory was called historical materialism. A truly classless society, in which all property is owned as a whole and everyone enjoys the same social and economic status, has never quite been achieved by proponents of Communism.

true overall equality. "From each according to their means, to each according to their needs" was the motto and guiding principle of the ideal Communist state.

MARX AND LENIN

In the nineteenth century, Karl Marx, the foremost intellectual proponent of Communism, believed that Communism would eventually occur naturally in the capitalist nations—although not without conflict and even violence—as wealth and property became too heavily concentrated in the hands of a small number of individuals, leaving the great mass of society relatively poor and impatient for change. He therefore predicted that Communism would come first to the richest capitalist nations of the world, especially those with a high degree of industrial development.

Vladimir Lenin speaks in Petrograd in April 1917. Whereas Marx believed that society would evolve to Communism after passing through the various economic stages, the last being industrial Communism, Lenin believed that Communism could be achieved without undergoing this process, and that the lower classes could achieve this revolutionary consciousness by being led by a ruling Communist government.

It did not happen that way, of course. Instead, the world's first successful Communist revolution took place in Russia in the last years of World War I (1914–1918). Far from being Europe's most prosperous independent nation, Russia was at the time one of its poorest and most backward, with very little industrial development at all. But Russia's Communists, especially Vladimir Lenin, argued that a small group or party of dedicated revolutionaries could seize power in a country and direct it toward Communism without necessarily passing through the other evolutionary stages of economic development, especially capitalism.

And this is what happened: a revolution in Russia in the years 1917 to 1918 led to the overthrow and murder of the Russian monarch (who was known as the czar) and the coming to power of Lenin's small

Communist party, the Bolsheviks. Without a single ally among the other nations of the world, Lenin and his comrades set out to overhaul Russian society from top to bottom to realize their vision of the ideal Communist state, the Union of Soviet Socialist Republics (USSR), known more simply as the Soviet Union. The upheaval, tumult, and suffering that this caused the Soviet people were tremendous, but by the end of World War II, the Soviet Union stood with the United States as the globe's two superpowers.

NORTH KOREA AND THE COLD WAR

More dangerous, from the U.S. point of view, was that many of the poorer and developing nations of the world now looked to the Soviet Union and Communism as a model for what they could achieve. From the Soviet point of view, despite the brief period of alliances with the United States and other capitalist countries during World War II, the capitalist countries had steadfastly opposed Communism from the beginning. When World War II ended, neither side trusted the other.

Although the armed forces of the United States, the Soviet Union, and their primary allies never opposed each other directly during the Cold War, the two superpowers indirectly engaged each other in military conflict on the battlefields of nations for whose loyalty they were competing. On several occasions, the Cold War conflict brought the world right to the edge of war between the United States and the Soviet Union with the most devastating weapons of mass destruction—nuclear weapons.

Although the Cold War is over, the Soviet Union is no more, and most of its constituent parts and satellite states have opted for independence, North Korea soldiers on, still proclaiming its belief in its own form of Communism and holding steadfastly to its antagonism toward the United States.

THE KOREAN PENINSULA

Korea is a narrow, relatively small peninsula in northeastern Asia. It juts southward from the easternmost flank of the huge country of China. Since 1948, the peninsula has been formally divided into two

Since the splitting of the Korean peninsula into two nations at the end of World War II, and further upon the armistice ending the Korean War in 1953, South Korea has achieved an economic growth that is eighteen times the level of North Korea's economic growth. The entire peninsula had been under Japanese rule for more than thirty-five years before the superpowers took control. The Military Demarcation Line, established at the time of the armistice, is 2.5 miles (4 km) wide and remains a "hot zone," with continuous military presence. South Korea still hopes to one day unify with North Korea.

THE KIM DYNASTY: NORTH KOREA'S GREATEST WEAPON

South Korean defense minister Cho Seong-tae (right) met with his North Korean counterpart, Kim Il Ch'ol (left) in their first ever talks in September 2000, in Seoul. The two vowed to aim for reducing the threat of war against one another.

In December 2002, at the height of tension between the United States and North Korea, Kim Il Ch'ol, defense minister for the Democratic People's Republic of Korea, announced that his country had a weapon more powerful than any atom bomb. This announcement, according to U.S. deputy secretary of state Richard Armitage, "threw us into a tizzy. We didn't understand what these weapons could be."

As it turned out, what the North Korean defense minister claimed was his country's most powerful weapon was "the single-hearted unity of the military and the people behind the invincible Commander Kim Jong Il." Kim Jong Il has ruled North Korea since 1994, when his father, Kim Il Sung, died. Kim Il Sung had ruled North Korea since 1948. The Kims are the only two rulers North Korea has known.

separate nations. Both of these nations maintain some claim to the rightful government of the entire peninsula.

The southern half of the peninsula is the nation formally named the Republic of Korea (ROK), commonly referred to simply as South Korea. The northern half is the nation formally named the Democratic

People's Republic of Korea (DPRK), commonly referred to simply as North Korea.

In size, North Korea is the slightly larger of the two, although it is significantly smaller in population. Its almost 23 million inhabitants refer to their nation, which is about the size of the state of Mississippi, as Choson. The slightly smaller South Korea, which is about the size of the state of Indiana, is home to more than twice as many people.

Nonetheless, South Korea's approximately 48 million inhabitants enjoy a much higher standard of living than North Koreans. Although at the time of the division, most of Korea's industry was located in the north, capitalist South Korea has since then far out-grown North Korea economically, making its economy one of Asia's strongest. Today, per capita income in South Korea is about twenty times as great as it is in Communist North Korea, in large part because of the close economic relations it maintains with the wealthy nations of Japan and the United States.

In contrast, the centrally directed economy of North Korea is stagnant and has been for decades. Even before the drought of 2000 that resulted in widespread famine, North Korea was dependent on international aid to feed its population. For years, a large number of North Koreans have suffered from malnutrition and even starvation. Despite this, the North Korean government has consistently devoted an enormous amount of resources to the military. It maintains a standing army of more than 1 million people. Even in recent years, as the nation has grown more diplomatically isolated and its economic situation has become increasingly desperate, the rulers of North Korea have placed an increased emphasis on the development of weapons of mass destruction, often in defiance of international treaty obligations.

The consistently tense relations between North Korea and South Korea, combined with the peninsula's location, make Korea a frequent focus of international attention and concern. North Korea shares a long northern border with the powerful Communist nation of China, a sometime ally. In the extreme northeastern portion of the country, North Korea shares a short but strategically important border with the southeasternmost region of Russia. To the east and the south, across the Sea of Japan from the Korean peninsula, is the island nation of Japan, which ruled Korea as a colony from 1906 to 1945. In places, Japan is little more than 100 miles (161 kilometers) from the Korean mainland.

DIVISION AND WAR

Independence for modern Korea came in August 1945, with the surrender of Japan to the United States, which brought about the end of World War II. Although Korea celebrated the end of Japanese rule, which had been brutal and much hated, Korea quickly became one of the first pawns in the Cold War chess game between the United States and the Soviet Union. With the defeat of the Japanese, both nations wanted to exert influence in Korea, and the country was soon divided. The Soviets occupied the peninsula north of the 38th parallel and helped establish a Communist government there, while the United States took the lead in occupying the south, helping establish a government friendly to its interests.

By 1948, both the Soviet Union and the United States had with-

drawn their troops from Korea, although both pledged continued support in the forms of economic and military aid to to the government they had established. North Korea also entered into agreements of alliance with China. Both North Korea and South Korea continued to claim that theirs should be the government for all of Korea.

On June 25, 1950, North Korean forces attacked South Korea, quickly overran most of the nation, including the capital, Seoul, and advanced as far south as Taegu. South Korea immediately asked the United Nations (UN) to condemn the aggression, which the UN did, ordering North Korea to withdraw back beyond the 38th parallel. When the North Koreans refused to do so, a huge UN coalition military

A U.S. soldier *(left)* trudges through a winter storm during the Korean War. The United States suffered approximately 44,000 fatalities in the conflict. This is a number slightly less than the number suffered in Vietnam, but during a much shorter span of time. A young girl *(above)* carries her brother past a U.S. M-26 tank in Haengju, South Korea, during the war. The United States maintains a military presence in South Korea today. South Korea's border with North Korea is one of the most heavily defended in the world.

force was assembled. The majority of the force was American, although troops from fifteen other nations also participated. Under the leadership of U.S. general Douglas MacArthur, the allied force counterattacked and advanced into the north. Defying President Harry Truman's orders to stop, MacArthur pressed forward recklessly, eventually advancing so far north that he provoked China into committing hundreds of thousands of troops into battle on North Korea's behalf.

President Harry Truman *(right)* is pictured here with General Douglas MacArthur *(left)* at their Wake Island meeting on October 15, 1950. Numerous theories abound as to the purpose of this meeting in the Pacific. One theory is that Truman wanted to remind MacArthur to keep the war limited and to end it quickly, while MacArthur thought the president was meeting for a political photo opportunity and purposefully dressed down for the meeting with the commander in chief he was known to criticize.

Now the overwhelmed allied force was driven relentlessly backward, far into the south, and Seoul fell to the North Koreans once again. MacArthur was dismissed by Truman and ordered home, and the allies once again drove the North Koreans back above the 38th parallel, where the war settled into a stalemate. The Soviet Union called for truce negotiations, and a peace agreement, formally establishing the boundary of the two nations at the 38th parallel, was signed on July 27, 1953, ending the Korean War. The two Koreas have lived in uneasy coexistence ever since. ■

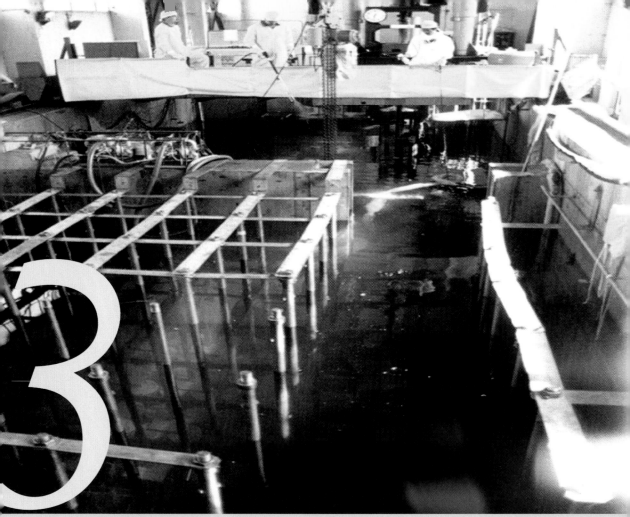

3 NORTH KOREA AND NUCLEAR WEAPONS

The most widely used definition of "weapons of mass destruction" in official U.S. government documents is "nuclear, chemical, or biological weapons." Many of these documents, such as the "National Strategy to Combat Weapons of Mass Destruction," a White House position paper produced in 2002, add another important criterion to the definition: that the weapons be in "the possession of hostile states and/or terrorists." This criterion is added to limit the discussion of WMD to enemies or potential enemies of the United States, but clearly the surest evidence as to whether a weapon properly fits into the category of WMD is its destructive potential, not who possesses it. In fact, to this day, there is little evidence that a terrorist group has ever succeeded in obtaining WMD as defined generally by the United States.

NUCLEAR WEAPONS: THE U.S. ARSENAL

In fact, the country with the most deadly arsenal of weapons of mass destruction is the United States. Although other countries, notably Russia, have larger stockpiles of weapons of mass destruction in certain specific categories, the U.S. arsenal is by far the most powerful, largely because the sophistication and variety of U.S. delivery devices give the U.S. military an unmatched flexibility and mobility of attack. In addition to land-based ballistic missiles, the United States can deliver WMD with cruise missiles; aerial drones and other unmanned aircraft; long-range bombers and other planes, aircraft carriers, destroyers, cruisers, and other ships; and, most important, on submarines known as SSBNs, or fleet ballistic missile submarines.

The United States has eighteen of these submarines, which it says provides the nation's most survivable and enduring nuclear strike capability. Ten of these submarines patrol the waters of the Atlantic; the other eight patrol the Pacific. Each carries twenty-four ballistic missiles, with each missile capable of carrying a number of nuclear warheads. These missiles can be delivered to specific targets from almost anywhere beneath the ocean's surface. The subs are the pride of the U.S. nuclear arsenal and perhaps the most envied part of any WMD program worldwide. What they mean to U.S. military strategists is that a sizable percentage—up to 50 percent—of the U.S. nuclear arsenal is in constant

Nuclear fuel rods are the source of nuclear energy in a reactor. Spent nuclear rods are highly radioactive, due to a buildup of plutonium and fission product, which makes the rods less and less effective. This is a photo released by North Korea, in February 2003, of spent fuel rods in a cooling pond. In 2004, North Korea claimed it reprocessed the plutonium from 8,000 spent fuel rods into nuclear weapons.

motion beneath the ocean's waves, meaning that it is essentially invulnerable to attack.

The United States is also the only nation that still deploys its nuclear weapons in foreign countries. As of 2000, the United States still had nuclear weapons stationed in Belgium, Germany, England, the Netherlands, Italy, Turkey, and Greece. At the height of the Cold War, the United States deployed thirty-eight nuclear weapons systems in twenty-seven countries or territories overseas, including South Korea.

NUCLEAR WEAPONS: A WORLD VIEW

As the above material suggests, the most feared type of WMD, and the one that most nations would most like to obtain, is nuclear

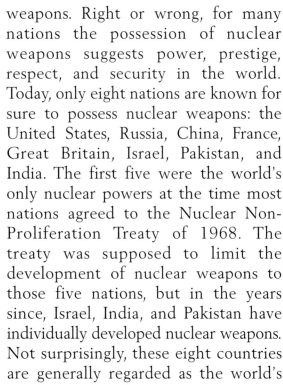

The USS *Florida* is one of four of the United States' ballistic missile submarines being converted into a guided missile submarine. Below: The *Florida* tests its new capabilities near the Bahamas, launching a Tomahawk cruise missile once submerged. The United States' sea-based arsenal is considered its main deterrent against attack. Sixteen percent of the total U.S. nuclear stockpile is believed to be at sea at any one time.

weapons. Right or wrong, for many nations the possession of nuclear weapons suggests power, prestige, respect, and security in the world. Today, only eight nations are known for sure to possess nuclear weapons: the United States, Russia, China, France, Great Britain, Israel, Pakistan, and India. The first five were the world's only nuclear powers at the time most nations agreed to the Nuclear Non-Proliferation Treaty of 1968. The treaty was supposed to limit the development of nuclear weapons to those five nations, but in the years since, Israel, India, and Pakistan have individually developed nuclear weapons. Not surprisingly, these eight countries are generally regarded as the world's most formidable military powers.

In recent years, many countries have exhibited a new interest in developing chemical and biological weapons. In large part, this is because developing such weapons is much less costly than starting and maintaining a nuclear program. However, no biological or chemical weapon yet developed has shown anywhere near the demonstrated destructive capacity of a nuclear weapon. Of the nations most active in developing nuclear weapons capacity, North Korea is generally believed to be the closest to actually creating a usable nuclear bomb. Some weapons analysts from the U.S. Central Intelligence Agency (CIA) even believe that North Korea may have succeeded in developing one or two nuclear weapons between 1989 and 1991.

A CHEMICAL WEAPON, TOO

It is also important to note that, in one important way, nuclear weapons also act as chemical weapons, in that the damage they do is not limited to the enormous destructive power of the initial blast. In the long term, radiation from the use of a nuclear weapon may do as much damage to human life as the initial blast. Although scientists still have much to learn about the effects of radiation on human health, it is clear that they are myriad and deadly. It is estimated that in the Japanese cities of Hiroshima and Nagasaki, where the United States dropped atomic bombs in August 1945, as many people may ultimately have died from the consequences of being exposed to radiation as from the immediate effects of the blast. According to the Federation of American Scientists (FAS), a group founded by scientists who had worked on the Manhattan Project (the successful U.S. effort to develop the atom bomb during World War II), "nuclear explosives have been the most feared of the weapons of mass destruction, in part because of their ability to cause enormous instantaneous devastation and [because] of the persistent effects of the radiation they emit, unseen and undetectable by unaided human senses."

> "Nuclear explosives have been the most feared of the weapons of mass destruction."
>
> *Federation of American Scientists*

NUCLEAR KOREA

It can be argued that both North and South Korea owe their existence to the success of the United States in becoming the first nation to

A crane lifts a bucket of concrete to the foundation of one of two nuclear reactors being built near the North Korean town of Kumho in August 2002. The building of these nuclear reactors was part of the agreement made by KEDO (Korean Peninsula Energy Development Organization), made up of Japan, South Korea, and the United States. The project, mostly paid for by South Korea, cost $5 billion. KEDO offered to build these reactors to keep North Korea in the nuclear pact it had made with the United States.

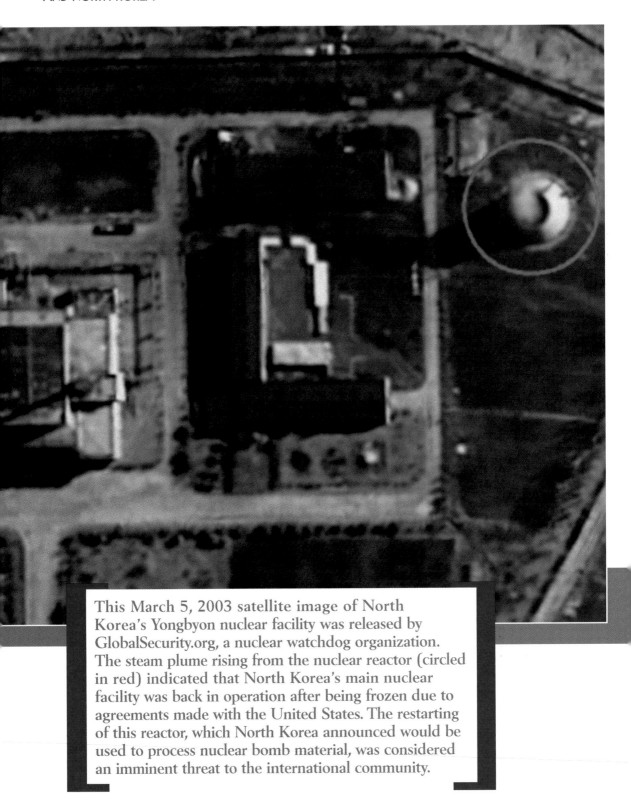

This March 5, 2003 satellite image of North Korea's Yongbyon nuclear facility was released by GlobalSecurity.org, a nuclear watchdog organization. The steam plume rising from the nuclear reactor (circled in red) indicated that North Korea's main nuclear facility was back in operation after being frozen due to agreements made with the United States. The restarting of this reactor, which North Korea announced would be used to process nuclear bomb material, was considered an imminent threat to the international community.

develop nuclear weapons. The atomic bombs that were dropped on Hiroshima and Nagasaki in August 1945 stunned the world with their destructive power and brought about the immediate surrender of Japan and the end of World War II. (The United States remains the only nation to have ever used a nuclear weapon against another nation.) One immediate consequence of Japan's surrender was Korea's independence from Japanese rule. Both North Korea and South Korea still celebrate Liberation Day as a national holiday.

During the Korean War, U.S. military commanders and political leaders considered using nuclear weapons against both North Korea and China. From the end of the war to the present day, the United States has maintained a large contingent of troops in South Korea, mostly concentrated along or near the 38th parallel, to secure its ally from attack from North Korea. From 1958 to 1991, the U.S. military presence there was bolstered by the deployment of a significant number and variety of nuclear weapons. In its ongoing dispute with the United States over its own WMD programs, North Korea sometimes claims that the United States is still maintaining 1,000 nuclear weapons in South Korea. There is, however, little evidence to support this claim.

FISSILE MATERIAL

The essential ingredient in developing a nuclear weapon is what is called fissile material. The simplest nuclear weapons are atomic bombs of the kind used by the United States against Japan. Such weapons work on the principle of nuclear fission.

Fission is the act of splitting or dividing. In a fission weapon, atoms of the fissile material are bombarded with neutrons, causing the nuclei of the fissile material to split, which releases the energy locked within. With a large enough mass of fissile material, the splitting nuclei set off a chain reaction of fission, resulting ultimately in the release of a tremendous amount of energy in the form of a devastating explosion. The necessary fissile material for such weapons are specific isotopes of the radioactive elements uranium and plutonium. These

TRAIN WRECK

On April 22, 2004, in the North Korean city of Ryongchon, about 30 miles (48 km) from the Chinese border, a train carrying chemicals exploded following a collision. The explosion leveled apartment buildings and a school in the vicinity; many young children were among the dead and injured. Eighteen hours later, massive black plumes of smoke from the explosion could still be seen from satellites in outer space, yet due to North Korea's isolation, details about the accident were difficult to come by even months after the tragedy.

Initially, the magnitude of the explosion led to suspicion that the train might have been carrying materials for North Korea's chemical or nuclear weapons programs, although that has proved not to be the case. Casualty figures have ranged from several hundred to several thousand. The accident made North

A South Korean convoy of Red Cross trucks carrying school supplies for North Korean schoolchildren was allowed to cross the border on May 7, 2004. The convoy was traveling to Ryongchon, North Korea, the site of the devastating train explosion.

Korea's poverty grimly evident to the rest of the world, as the Kim government sent out emergency pleas for such basic medical necessities as bandages, blankets, syringes, and antibiotics. Even so, North Korea remained suspicious of those offering help, refusing to allow South Korean trucks and ships bearing emergency medical and food supplies to cross into its territory and initially turning down U.S. offers of assistance. The suspicion with which the North Korean government responded to offers of assistance in the wake of the tragedy give some indication of the secrecy that has proved to be such a source of frustration to those who have attempted to negotiate with the North Koreans about WMD and other issues.

materials are called fissile because they split into relatively equal masses when hit even by low-energy neutrons.

FUSION

Fusion weapons, such as the hydrogen bomb, generate their much greater explosive force from the joining together of nuclei (fusion) rather than splitting apart nuclei (fission). In these thermonuclear devices, the fusion of the nuclei of isotopes of hydrogen, deuterium, and tritium result in the release of energy in the form of a tremendous explosion. Even fusion weapons, however, require fissile material. The energy, heat, and pressure that result from the fission explosion of the necessary uranium or plutonium isotopes are used to trigger the fusion of the other elements and create an even larger explosion. Essentially, a fission reaction is used to trigger the fusion explosion.

ENRICHMENT

The first step for a nation wishing to develop nuclear weapons, there-fore, is to obtain an adequate supply of fissile material. Scientists

Remolded uranium is held here in gloved hands after being removed from a U.S. Titan II missile in compliance with a disarmament treaty during the Cold War. Greater amounts of uranium naturally occur on Earth than does plutonium. Yet uranium can be bred to produce the more coveted weapons-grade plutonium by nuclear fission.

agree that this is the most crucial part of the process. That fissile material must then be "enriched," or separated from less fissile isotopes of the element, because only an extremely small percentage of uranium ore, for example, contains fissile isotopes. Although the enrichment process requires extremely sophisticated machinery and a considerable amount of scientific and technological expertise, analysts agree that many nations possess the necessary know-how, provided they can assure themselves of a sufficient and reliable supply of fissile material.

URANIUM

Uranium is the critical fissile material. Plutonium contains an even greater energy-producing potential, but there is not enough of it in nature for nuclear weapons or even nuclear energy programs. Instead, it must be made in a nuclear reactor by being bombarded with neutrons from a uranium fission chain reaction.

It was once thought that uranium was also exceedingly rare in nature, but scientists now know that it is actually as or more plentiful than several common elements, such as mercury, antimony, molybdenum, arsenic, and even silver. It can be found in numerous minerals and even in phosphate rock, which is relatively common.

North Korea has a number of uranium mines, with an estimated reserve of 4 million tons of high-quality uranium. Only a small percentage of that ore—less than 1 percent—could be enriched for use as fissile material, but this would still provide North Korea with more than enough material for several weapons, although it is uncertain how advanced the country's refining and processing equipment is.

NUKES IN NORTH KOREA?

What is certain is that in the almost sixty years of the nation's existence, North Korea's only two leaders, Kim Il Sung and his son, Kim Jong Il, who succeeded him in 1994, have expressed a consistent interest in developing nuclear weapons, although they have erratically pursued that goal. Experts on North Korea are not sure whether the two Kims' motivation in developing such weapons is aggressive in nature (that is, to menace neighbors, primarily South Korea, and enemies such as the United States) or essentially defensive as a result of feeling threatened by, for example, the presence of U.S. forces and nuclear weapons in South Korea. It is also possible that the two Kims have used North Korea's nuclear weapons program as a kind of bargaining chip with the outside world, a sometimes successful tactic that some analysts refer to as nuclear blackmail.

For example, several times since 1990, North Korea has hinted or even stated outright that it has nuclear weapons. When concerned outside powers, such as the United States, react with the expected alarm, North

Kim Il Sung, the founder of North Korea, is pictured here with his son, Kim Jong Il, in this 1983 photograph taken at a celebration in Pyongyang, marking the founding of this Communist nation. The elder Kim had been a member of the Korean Communist Party in 1925. When it disbanded, he joined the Chinese Communist Party and returned to Korea with the Soviet occupation at the end of World War II. He was appointed prime minister of the DPRK by the Soviets in 1948.

Korea offers "concessions." Such concessions may come in the form of allowing UN arms inspectors to examine its facilities or promising to halt work on weapons programs in exchange for outside aid that it desperately needs and would otherwise be unable to obtain, such as parts and fuel for nuclear reactors that provide power for its impoverished people.

As has generally been true of its relationship with the outside world, North Korea's behavior regarding its nuclear weapons program has been secretive, inconsistent, and unreliable. For example, North Korea signed the Nuclear Non-Proliferation Treaty in 1985, only to threaten to withdraw from it in 1993. In the 1970s and early 1980s, it agreed to UN inspections of its nuclear reactors, only to rescind such approval in the early 1990s. In 1991, it reached an agreement with South Korea stipulating that the Korean peninsula was to remain free of nuclear weapons, and allowing for mutual inspections of each others' facilities, but in succeeding years it refused to allow inspectors access to its facilities. In 1994, North Korea threatened to use nuclear weapons to turn Seoul into a "sea of fire" but then reached an agreement with the United States known as the joint framework. The agreement provided for various forms of U.S. economic concessions and aid in exchange for North Korea's agreement to freeze all development of nuclear weapons. However, in 2002, North Korea then claimed that it had a secret program to enrich uranium for nuclear weapons—a direct violation of the joint framework. Less than a year later, North Korea stated outright that it had nuclear weapons and would develop more unless the United States agreed to direct negotiations aimed at providing more economic aid.

It is difficult, if not impossible, to know with any certainty the exact status of North Korea's nuclear weapons program. What is certain is that North Korea is interested in developing nuclear weapons, if only to use as a bargaining chip with outside powers, particularly the United States. North Korea's uranium mines do provide it with a reliable native source of fissile material sufficient to develop some weapons. The country also has nuclear reactors, which are largely reliant on old Soviet technology, apparently capable of enriching uranium and even producing some weapons-grade plutonium. It has received information

A North Korean soldier begs for food from Chinese tourists on a boat from a nearby bordering town. China seeks to end illegal immigration of North Koreans trying to escape famine, economic hardship, and oppression in North Korea. China provides North Korea with 70 percent of its food and oil imports, and pledged $1.2 million to the ailing nation after the train disaster in Ryongchon.

and technology from Pakistan, a developing nation that has succeeded in developing nuclear weaponry. It has a fairly advanced missile technology program that exports ballistic missile technology to several other countries, and has deployed an estimated total of 500 to 600 ballistic missiles of its own production. At present, the range of North Korea's missiles make them a danger only to its immediate neighbors, not the continental United States, though missile systems in production in North Korea are feared to have the potential to reach Alaska.

Even so, and despite its own claims and the CIA's belief that it may have once developed one or two nuclear bombs, most analysts believe that North Korea has not actually succeeded in developing viable nuclear weapons, mainly because there is little evidence of the country conducting successful tests of such weaponry. Needless to say, tests of weapons of such explosive power are extremely difficult to conceal, especially from sophisticated satellite surveillance technology such as that possessed by the United States. ■

4

BIOLOGICAL AND CHEMICAL WEAPONS IN NORTH KOREA

For all their terrifying potential, biological and chemical weapons have never demonstrated the same deadly impact as nuclear weapons. Chemical weapons have been used on the battlefield only a handful of times— most notably by the Germans during the trench warfare of World War I; by the Italians during Fascist dictator

Italian dictator Benito Mussolini demonstrates a new type of gas bomb to his military officials in Rome in 1935. Italian forces were the first to drop mustard gas bombs using airplanes on Ethiopia, Africa's oldest independent nation, which Italy then occupied from 1936 to 1941. World opinion turned against the Fascist dictator for this action, who then joined forces with Adolf Hitler, making Italy an Axis power in World War II.

Benito Mussolini's invasion of Ethiopia in 1936; by the Japanese against the Chinese in the northern mainland region of Manchuria during the lead-up to World War II in 1936 and 1937; by the Iraqis against the Iranians in the war between those two countries in the 1980s; and by Iraq against its Kurdish population in the same decade. Of all these cases, Saddam Hussein's attack on the Kurds with chemical weapons caused the greatest damage. The gases and other weaponized chemical agents proved volatile and extremely hard to handle and use; in World War I, when the wind changed direction, they came back against the German soldiers who had launched them. A poison gas attack by a bizarre Japanese cult, Aum Shinrikyo, in the Tokyo subway system in 1995 resulted in twelve deaths, far from the mayhem the cult had hoped to unleash.

U.S. soldiers inspect a truck for possible chemical weapons in a military exercise near the demilitarized zone between North Korea and South Korea. It is estimated that North Korea has as much as 4,500 tons of chemical weapons, with the capability of producing 12,000 tons per year in case of war.

Biological weapons have a more brief history. To this point in time, there is no record of biological agents being used successfully as a weapon of war by a country or group against a foreign enemy.

Despite this record, governments continue to display an interest in developing chemical and biological weapons as part of their countries' military arsenals. In recent years, this trend has grown stronger, perhaps because such weapons are seen as much cheaper alternatives to nuclear weapons. Advances in techniques and technology, such as genetic engineering, have also offered the possibility of new breakthroughs with such weapons.

WHAT IS A BIOLOGICAL WEAPON?

Any general who has ever commanded an army in a long, drawn-out campaign, particularly on foreign soil or terrain, knows that disease can prove as great a threat to troops as the enemy. Throughout history, there are countless examples of the ranks of invading armies being decimated by epidemics of infectious diseases. One such example involved the Nazi German troops during the five-month Battle of Stalingrad, where more lives were claimed than in any other single conflict of World War II. Exposed to the elements, living in close quarters, often poorly fed and without access to adequate sanitary facilities and medical care, soldiers on campaign are natural prey for the infectious biological agents that cause disease. Sometimes, too, it is the invaders who bring disease to the native population, as when the European settlers and conquerors of the New World devastated Native American populations of the Americas by exposing them to diseases for which they had no immunity, especially the deadly scourge of smallpox.

Perhaps it was in the course of one of these historic episodes that the idea of trying to harness germs and microbes as military weapons was born. Several different Native American peoples in North America certainly believed that they were intentionally exposed to smallpox in the course of trade with Europeans. Most often, the story goes, the smallpox virus was on the blankets the Native Americans coveted in trade from the Europeans. There are similar stories and allegations told and made by the peoples of other cultures as well. The stories are impossible to verify

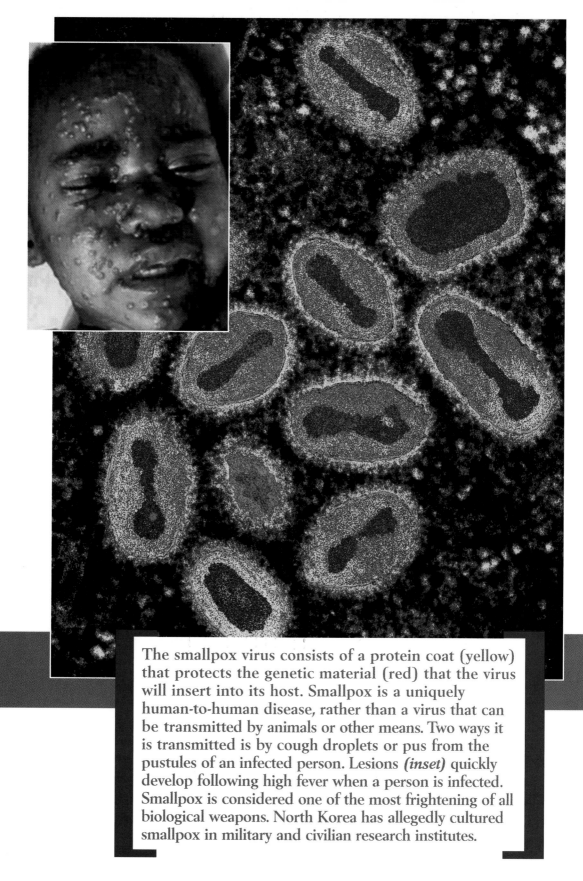

The smallpox virus consists of a protein coat (yellow) that protects the genetic material (red) that the virus will insert into its host. Smallpox is a uniquely human-to-human disease, rather than a virus that can be transmitted by animals or other means. Two ways it is transmitted is by cough droplets or pus from the pustules of an infected person. Lesions *(inset)* quickly develop following high fever when a person is infected. Smallpox is considered one of the most frightening of all biological weapons. North Korea has allegedly cultured smallpox in military and civilian research institutes.

today, but if true, they would have marked the early use of biological agents as weapons of war.

Biological warfare may be understood as the intentional spreading of disease-causing agents as a weapon against an enemy military force or civilian population, with the goal of causing large numbers of that group to sicken or die. In general, such biological agents fall into the following categories:

■ Bacteria are small free-living organisms that can cause disease. If you've ever received a prescription of antibiotics to treat an illness, your doctor believes you're suffering from a sickness caused by bacteria. The bubonic plague, also known as the black death, is an example of a deadly disease caused by bacteria.

NORTH KOREA'S BIOLOGICAL WEAPONS: THE STATE DEPARTMENT'S VIEW

On May 7, 2002, John R. Bolton, the U.S. undersecretary of state for Arms Control and International Security, described North Korea's biological arms program in testimony to the U.S. Senate:

North Korea has a dedicated, national-level effort to achieve a [biological weapons] capability and has developed and produced, and may have weaponized [biological] agents . . . Despite the fact that its citizens are starving, the leadership has spent large sums of money to acquire the resources, including a biotechnology infrastructure, capable of producing infectious agents, toxins, and other crude biological weapons. It likely has the capability to produce sufficient quantities of biological agents for military purposes within weeks of deciding to do so, and has a variety of means at its disposal for delivering these deadly weapons.

■ Viruses are organisms that require the cell of another organism in order to replicate. They thus become dependent on the cells of the host organism. Many of the most deadly epidemics in history, such as smallpox, were caused by viruses.

■ Rickettsiae are microorganisms that have characteristics of both bacteria (they often respond to treatment with antibiotics) and of viruses (they grow only in the cells of other organisms). Typhus is an example of a particularly deadly disease caused by rickettsiae.

■ Fungi are small spore-forming organisms, some of which can cause disease.

■ Toxins are poisonous substances produced or derived from living things. Botulism is an example of a deadly disease caused by a toxin.

South Korean soldiers patrol near the demilitarized zone along the border with North Korea. Hostile relations with North Korea cause South Korea to keep as close a watch as possible on North Korea's WMD. Though South Korea believes its neighbor has weaponized two biological agents, a biological attack is considered unlikely as North Korea could be affected as well.

A South Korean antibioterror police squad arrives at a boutique department store in Seoul to exercise preparedness for a biological or chemical attack in anticipation of the 2002 FIFA World Cup that the nation was hosting. The last eruption of hostilities between North Korea and South Korea was brief gun battles between the two navies. Many South Koreans are frustrated with the United States' influence in South Korea, seeing it as a roadblock to unification with the north as U.S. negotiations are judged as being too harsh toward the north.

NORTH KOREA'S BIOLOGICAL WEAPONS PROGRAM

North Korea has been actively developing a biological weapons program since the early 1960s, often hand in hand with its chemical weapons program. According to Pak Tong-Sam, a South Korean defense analyst, in 1964 Kim Il Sung directed the "concentrated development of biological weapons," having decided that "poisonous gas and bacteria can be used effectively in war."

Although precise details about North Korea's program are difficult to establish, South Koreans believe that North Korea experimented with approximately a dozen different biological agents as weapons of mass destruction, including

51

the causative agents for smallpox, cholera, plague, typhus, yellow fever, tuberculosis, and anthrax before concentrating on producing biological weapons from just a few agents in the 1980s. Most analysts believe that since then, North Korea has concentrated on producing weapons that would cause anthrax, botulism, smallpox, and the plague, with a particular emphasis on one or two agents from that group.

Once weapons-grade, disease-causing agents are produced, they must be "weaponized," meaning they are placed in the shells, bombs, or warheads by which they will be delivered. The delivery systems for North Korea's biological weapons are generally artillery shells and missile warheads. South Korean analysts believe that half of North Korea's long-range missiles and 30 percent of its artillery pieces are equipped to deliver biological weapons. South Korea also alleges that there are anywhere from three to ten production and research facilities for biological weapons in North Korea. The United States believes that North Korea has the ability to produce, at short notice, large quantities of weapons-grade biological agents, with a somewhat lesser capacity for rapid weaponization and delivery.

WHAT IS A CHEMICAL WEAPON?

As defined by the Federation of American Scientists, a chemical weapon is one that uses the toxic or poisonous properties of a chemical substance, rather than its explosive properties, to inflict damage on an enemy. Although technological advances have made chemical weapons more attractive to some nations as potential weapons of mass destruction, their successful use on the battlefield still remains relatively infrequent, perhaps because they are difficult to control and require the forces using them to also take extensive protective measures.

In general, chemical weapons fall into the following categories:

■ Vesicants, or blistering agents, cause burns and blistering to the skin even at low doses of exposure. The best-known chemical weapon of this kind is mustard gas, which was used by the Germans in World War I and the Iraqis in the Iran-Iraq War of the 1980s. Mustard gas is difficult to detect and causes no injuries

A soldier collapses to the ground after inhaling fumes in a gas attack during World War I on a battlefield in France in 1918. Chemical warfare was introduced in World War I, and was then made illegal by a series of treaties that culminated into the Geneva Protocol in 1925. Yet since this was not enforced, chemical warfare was again used in World War II.

upon initial contact with the skin. Burns and blisters take hours after contact to appear.

■ Choking agents cause irritation of the eyes and difficulty breathing. Common chemical weapons of this kind are chlorine and phosgene.

■ Blood agents interfere with the ability of the blood to transfer oxygen to the tissues and cells, often resulting in rapid unconsciousness or death. Hydrogen cyanide and arsine are examples of blood agents.

■ Nerve agents are liquids initially developed for use as pesticides. They are the most lethal type of chemical weapons and cause injury and death when inhaled or absorbed through the skin. The most well-known and toxic are tabun (known also as GA) and sarin (known also as GB). Both were developed by the Germans shortly before World War II.

■ V agents are particularly toxic when they come in contact with the skin, which interested weapons designers because they thus rendered gas masks ineffective. The best known is VX gas.

The chief delegates of six-party talks held in June 2004 head to a meeting in Beijing. The delegates represent (from left to right) South Korea, China, the United States, North Korea, Japan, and Russia. This particular round of negotiations saw no concrete success in persuading North Korea to roll back its nuclear weapons program if offered the right incentives, yet all parties remain intent on reaching a solution of peace.

NORTH KOREA'S CHEMICAL WEAPONS PROGRAM

In many ways, North Korea's chemical weapons program is the most advanced of its WMD programs. Since Kim Il Sung's 1964 directive about biological and chemical weapons, North Korea has amassed one of the world's largest stockpiles of chemical weapons. This stockpile is estimated to consist of between 2,500 to 5,000 tons of sarin, tabun, phosgene, mustard gas, and hydrogen cyanide. These chemical agents are made in at least eight separate production facilities and stocked in six different storage facilities and more than 150 mountain tunnels in the country's interior. In addition, the North Korean civilian population is well trained in protective measures if they are attacked by a foreign enemy with chemical weapons.

Chemical weapons can be delivered with missiles, aerial bombs, rockets, and artillery shells. A significant percentage of North Korea's chemical weapons arsenal is weaponized, or already filled into artillery shells, rocket, and missile warheads. North Korea has literally thousands of artillery pieces capable of delivering chemical weapons within 100 miles (161 km) of the 38th parallel. That number has increased significantly in the past few years.

CONCLUSION: A SIGNIFICANT THREAT?

So how great a danger are North Korea's weapons of mass destruction? Does North Korea deserve designation as a rogue state, a member of the axis of evil? Certainly in its brief history it has displayed erratic leadership, an indifference to world opinion, and a consistent hostility to the United States, although since the Korean War it has not been able to do much more than bluster and posture to express its discontent. In all likelihood, it will continue to use the threat of further development of WMD as a bargaining tool to gain the aid it so desperately needs. It has little else to bargain with, and it would have little to gain by launching an aggressive action against any of its neighbors. In any event, in such an unsettled world, North Korea will certainly be closely watched by the United States and others for any sign that it is accelerating any of its WMD programs. ∎

[GLOSSARY]

Al Qaeda A network of Islamic extremists, organized by Saudi Arabian Osama bin Laden, whose ultimate goal is to establish a great Islamic kingdom. Al Qaeda, which means "the base" in Arabic, carries out operations against pro-Western governments in Muslim regions and seeks to drive out Western presence at Islamic holy sites.

atheist One who does not believe in the existence of a god.

blackmail An extortion of payment in exchange for something precious to the person being blackmailed.

Bolsheviks Name for the faction of the Russian Social Democratic Labor Party led by Vladimir Lenin. The Bolsheviks seized power during the Russian Revolution of 1917 and became the All-Russian Communist Party. "Bolshevik" is derived from a Russian word that loosely means "majority."

Choson The Korean name for the Asian peninsula that separates the Yellow Sea and the Sea of Japan. Originally used to refer to the last traditional kingdom that ended in 1910, when the peninsula became a Japanese province, it is now the term used by North Koreans to refer to their nation.

clandestine Conducted in secret.

criterion A standard upon which a judgment will be based.

Democratic People's Republic of Korea (DPRK) The official name of the northern half of the Korean peninsula, established in 1948 as North Korea.

electorate The body of people entitled to vote.

Fascist A person who believes in Fascism. Fascism is a system of government where nation and race are of greater importance than the individual. Often used in referring to the government of Benito Mussolini, it comes from the Italian word *fascio*, meaning "bundle" or "group." Mussolini was the dictator of this centralized, autocratic form of government in Italy from 1922 to 1943.

isotope Any of two or more atoms of the same element that have different atomic masses yet the same atomic number.

Liberation Day In North Korea and South Korea, the holiday celebrated on August 15 that marks the surrender of Japan at the end of World War II and the establishment of both North Korea and South Korea.

myriad Innumerable.

Nuclear Non-Proliferation Treaty of 1968 The most widely accepted arms-control treaty that prohibits nuclear weapon states from transferring any type of nuclear material to non–nuclear weapon states. In return, non–nuclear weapon states that have signed the treaty agree not to acquire or produce nuclear weaponry.

peninsula A piece of land surrounded by water on all sides but one.

proliferate To produce rapidly, increasing in numbers.

relic A remainder of a past custom or practice.

Republic of Korea The official name of the republic known as South Korea, established in 1948. South Koreans refer to their nation as Han'guk.

rescind To take back.

rogue Dishonest or unprincipled; living apart from others.

territory A geographical area under the jurisdiction of an external government but possessing some autonomy.

thermonuclear Relating to the very high temperatures obtained by the fission process to ignite the fusion process of atoms with a low atomic weight, such as hydrogen atoms.

uranium A radioactive metallic element used as a source of atomic energy.

FOR MORE INFORMATION

The Carnegie Endowment for International Peace
1779 Massachusetts Avenue NW
Washington, DC 20036-2103
(202) 483-7600
Web site: http://www.ceip.org

The Nuclear Threat Initiative
1747 Pennsylvania Avenue NW, 7th Floor
Washington, DC 20006
(202) 296-4810

WEB SITES

Due to the changing nature of Internet links, the Rosen Publishing Group, Inc., has developed an online list of Web sites related to the subject of this book. This site is updated regularly. Please use this link to access the list:

http://www.rosenlinks.com/lwmd/wmdnk

[FOR FURTHER] READING

Kim, Kyoung-Soo. *North Korea's Weapons of Mass Destruction: Problems and Prospects*. Elizabeth, NJ: Hollym International Corporation, 2004.

McGowen, Tom. *The Korean War.* New York: Franklin Watts, 1992.

Payan, Gregory. *Chemical and Biological Weapons: Anthrax and Sarin.* New York: Scholastic, 2000.

Streissguth, Thomas. *Nuclear Weapons: More Countries, More Threats.* Berkeley Heights, NJ: Enslow Publishers, 2000.

BIBLIOGRAPHY

Carnegie Endowment for International Peace. "Carnegie Non-Proliferation Project: North Korea Nuclear and Missile Timeline." Retrieved June 8, 2004 (http://www.ceip.org/files/projects/npp/resources/koreatimeline.htm).

Carnegie Endowment for International Peace. "The Nuclear Non-Proliferation Treaty." Retrieved June 8, 2004 (http://www.ceip.org/files/projects/npp/resources/npttext.htm).

Disarmament.org. "Weapons of Mass Destruction Branch Department for Disarmament Affairs." Retrieved June 8, 2004 (http://disarmament.un.org:8080/wmd).

The Federation of American Scientists. "WMD Around the World: North Korea: Biological Weapons Program." Retrieved June 8, 2004 (http://www.fas.org/nuke/guide/dprk/bw/index.html).

The Federation of American Scientists. "WMD Around the World: North Korea: Chemical Weapons Program." Retrieved June 8, 2004 (http://www.fas.org/nuke/guide/dprk/cw/index.html).

The Federation of American Scientists. "WMD Around the World: North Korea: Nuclear Weapons Program." Retrieved June 8, 2004 (http://www.fas.org/nuke/guide/dprk/nuke/index.html).

Gaddis, John Lewis. *We Now Know: Rethinking the Cold War.* New York: Oxford University Press, 1997.

Levine, Herbert M. *Chemical and Biological Weapons in Our Time.* Danbury, CT: Franklin Watts, 2000.

Malkasian, Carter. *The Korean War.* Oxford, England: Osprey Publishing, 2001.

Marx, Karl, and Friedrich Engels. *The Communist Manifesto.* New York: Simon & Schuster, 1964.

Miller, Debra A., ed. *North Korea.* Farmington Hills, MI: Greenhaven Press, 2004.

MissileThreat.com. "What Is a Ballistic Missile?" Retrieved June 8, 2004 (http://www.missilethreat.com/overview/bm.html).

The Nuclear Threat Initiative. "North Korea Profile." Retrieved June 8, 2004 (http://www.nti.org/e_research/profiles/NK/index.html).

Triplett, William C. *Rogue State: How a Nuclear North Korea Threatens America*. Washington, DC: Regency Publishing 2004.

The World Factbook. "Korea, North." Retrieved June 8, 2004 (http://www.cia.gov/cia/publications/factbook/geos/kn.html).

The World Factbook. "Korea, South." Retrieved June 8, 2004 (http://www.cia.gov/cia/publications/factbook/geos/ks.html).

[INDEX]

ABOUT THE AUTHOR

Tracie Egan is the author of several nonfiction young adult books on subjects ranging from team sports to American political history. She majored in graphic design and journalism at New York University, and is currently an editor at the women's magazine *Bust*. As a New York City resident, terrorism and weapons of mass destruction are of great concern to her, and researching this book shed light on some of her unanswered questions about these issues.

PHOTO CREDITS

Cover, title page, pp. 4–5, 28, 33, 44, 49, 50–51, 54 AP/Wide World Photos; p. 7 © Brooks Kraft/Corbis; p. 9 © Mian Khursheed/Reuters/Corbis; pp. 10–11 © 2002 Geoatlas; p. 14 © Hulton Archive/Getty Images; p. 16 Franklin D. Roosevelt Library; p. 18 Archives Charmet/Bridgeman Art Library; p. 19 Collection Kharbine-Tapabor, Paris/Bridgeman Art Library; p. 21 Library of Congress, Geography and Map Division; pp. 22, 40, 47 (inset) © Reuters/Corbis; pp. 24, 25 National Archives and Records Administration; pp. 26, 30–31, 31 (inset), 34, 45, 53 © Getty Images; p. 36 © Jean Chung/Corbis; p. 38 © Martin Marietta, Roger Ressmeyer/Corbis; p. 42 © Wilson Chu/Reuters/Corbis; p. 47 Eye of Science/Photo Researchers, Inc.

Designer: Evelyn Horovicz; Editor: Leigh Ann Cobb;
Photo Researcher: Jeffrey Wendt